The Story of Standing Rock

by Diana Crow-Wheel and Dawn Admire-Sanders
Copyright © 2017 Diana Crow-Wheel., Everfield Press, Florida. Publication date October 27, 2017. All rights reserved. No part of this book shall be reproduced or transmitted in any form or means, electronic, mechanical, magnetic, photographic including photocopying, recording or by any information storage and retrieval system, without prior written permission of the author.
All rights reserved.
ISBN
978-1-946785-03-9

The Story of Standing Rock

by
Diana Crow-Wheel
and
Dawn Admire-Sanders

Forward by
LaDonna Bravebull Allard

1.

DEDICATION
For those who stood at Standing Rock and for the supporters who made it possible.
2016-2017

Sacred Stone was established April 1, 2016 to stand in prayer and resistance against an oil company. We stood up for the water, for life and for the next generation. The cry went out across the world "Mni Wiconi" which means "Water is Life" by the youth. The youth answered the call for the water. They put their feet on the ground and ran with prayer to wake up the world.

Standing Rock was only the seed that needs to grow across the world to change our lives for the better.

Can you hear our call, "Mni Wiconi"… "Water is Life"?

LaDonna BraveBull Allard
Tamaka Waste Win
Good Earth Woman
November 12, 2017

"I see a time of seven generations when all colors of mankind will gather under the sacred tree of life and the whole earth will become one circle again."

~ Crazy Horse

4.

A Native American Prophecy said a bad black snake would come across our land in America. They named it Zuzeca Sape.

5.

The black snake is the oil pipeline!

6.

This black snake would go under the big Missouri River.

7.

So many languages and people recognized this prophecy. It was as if the water touched them and they listened.

8.

If you stand still by the riverside and listen with your heart, the water will remember you.
The water will remind you it is important for...

9.

people...

10.

animals...

trees and plants…

12.

fish and more!

13.

The water in North Dakota needed helping hands.

14.

A woman from the Standing Rock Sioux Tribe knew this, and asked people to come and help stop the black snake.

15.

Her name was...
LaDonna Bravebull Allard.

16.

She asked people to come protect the water and pray to stop the black snake.

17.

A lot of people came to the camps.

18.

They brought tipis to live in.

19.

Children came to help and made friends!

20.

Horses came to help and made friends!

21.

Dogs came to help and made friends!

22.

People from all over the world came to help and made friends! They all came to...

23.

show their support to stop the black snake.

24.

These were the rules at camp.

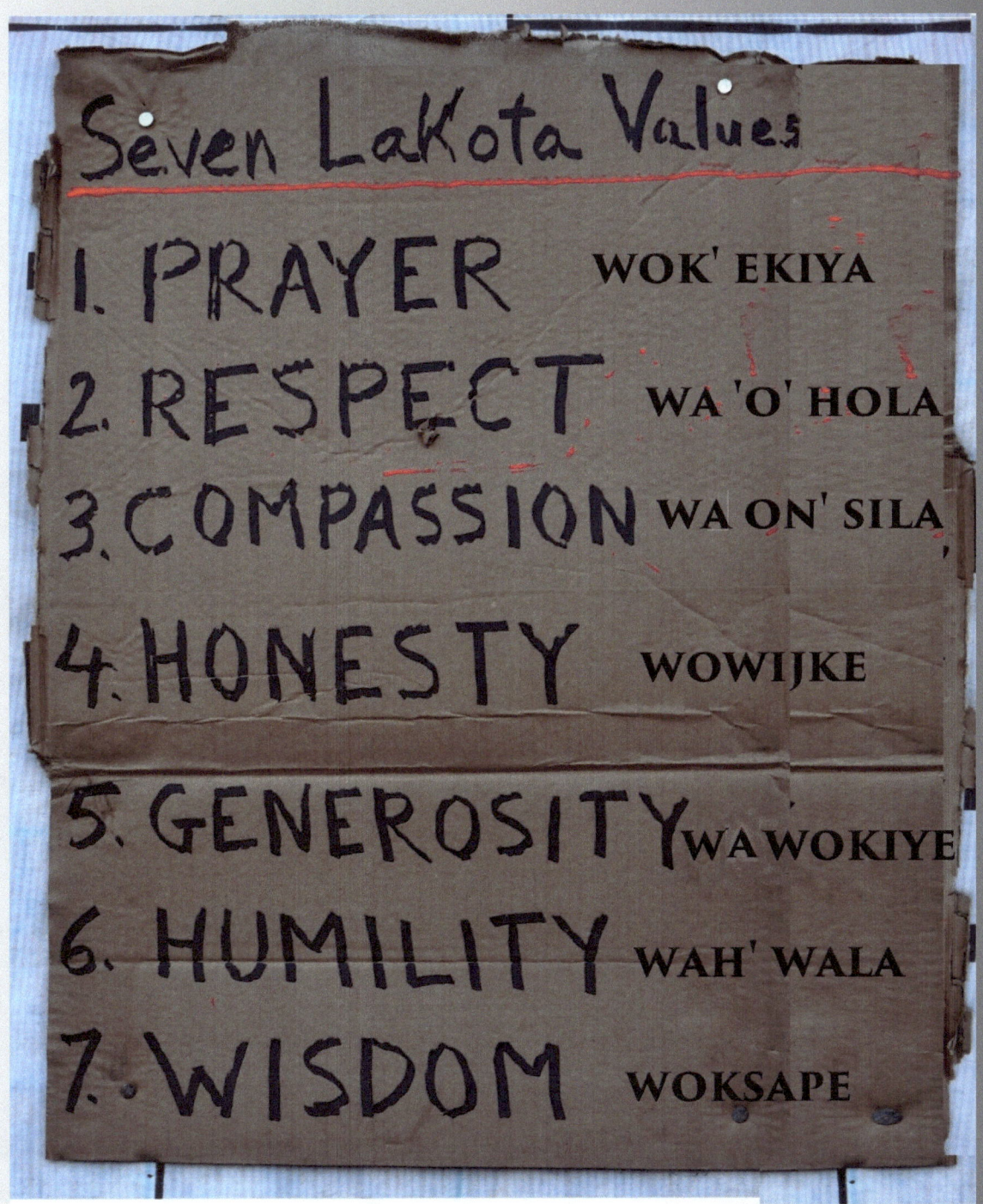

This was the largest gathering of native people and their friends anyone could remember, ever.

26.

They prayed peacefully.

27.

They were called to stop the black snake.

28.

They were called to become water protectors.

29.

"Mni Wiconi" means...

30.

They collected sunshine with solar panels to make power for their lights and phones.

31.

They made a community schoolhouse with mud and straw.

32.

They gathered to show...
"We Will Not Be Silent!"

33.

The veterans came to help.

34.

The holy people came to help.

35.

The doctors, nurses, and healers came to help.

36.

Sadly, the black snake went under the Missouri River.

37.

People prayed that the black snake would not leak oil into the sacred waters.

38.

Water protectors left Standing Rock to teach others.

They told the story of Standing Rock.

40.

They told people how to stop the black snake.

41.

They told people how we can use the sun for energy instead of using oil.

42.

They told people how we can use the wind for energy instead of using oil.

43.

They told us there is always hope. Someday the black snake will stop drinking oil and get energy from the sun.

44.

Charles Recountre created his sculpture 'Not Afraid to Look' at Standing Rock. This sculpture looks in the face of all that was. It reminds us there is always hope.

It reminds us that we can stand still, listen, and look with our hearts. Then the water will remember us. The water will remind us.

http://www.publicartarchive.org/work/not-afraid-look

The water will remind you that you can be a water protector too!

46.

You can tell others "Mni Wiconi".
This means Water is Life!

47.

Diana Crow-Wheel is the author and a teacher and artist. She is also a Water Protector and Activist for the Earth. She stands among the many women, mothers and grandmothers who carry the medicine of the water.

Dawn Admire-Sanders is the co-author. She was a key board warrior for Standing Rock, a mom and an activist. She lives in Florissant, Colorado.

Dr. Cauhilla Red Elk, is a CEO at the Center On Human Rights Advocacy and American Indian Law in Colorado Springs, Colorado. She has been a supportive voice in this project.

Each picture of this story can tell another story. The tipis were built by those who love the earth. The paintings and drawings were painted by those that love the earth. The statue of Crazy Horse has a history that can teach those who listen. The pipeline has a history each one of us needs to learn. The people who numbered in the thousands came from so far to share in this effort.

They left their mark in the heart of all of us. The animals, children, and people made so many friends that will not be forgotten. The only thing left when the land was cleared was the statue "Not Afraid to Look". There is another sculpture like this in Santa Fe, New Mexico. Thank you for all who keep the spirit of this effort to save the Water!

Image Credits:
1, 3,4,5,6,8, 9, 10, 11, 14, 15, 17, 19, 24, 25, 26, 27, 28, 29, 30, 31, 33, 36, 37, 38, 39, 40, 42, 43, 44, 45, 47 Diana Crow-Wheel,
2, 7, 12, 13 Lyra Raine Sanders and Ryder James Sanders,
10 Halley Ya-Hua Vincent, 18 Alisha Vincent,
19 Iggy Igloo, 18,20 Maggie Desbiens,
21,32 Mitra Singh, 22 Dan Nanamkin, 19,23,40 Lola Davis,
35 Public image, 34 Kash Jackson,
41,46 Dawn Admire-Sanders,
43 Summer Bauer

50.

www.ingramcontent.com/pod-product-compliance
Lightning Source LLC
Chambersburg PA
CBHW041505220426
43661CB00016B/1259